SECOND EDITION

¡ADELANTE! UNO

An Invitation to Spanish

José A. Blanco

VISTA®
HIGHER LEARNING

Boston, Massachusetts

Publisher: José A. Blanco

President: Janet Dracksdorf

Editorial Development: Deborah Coffey, Jo Hanna Kurth

Project Management: Maria Rosa Alcaraz, Natalia González Peña, Hillary Gospodarek, Sharon Inglis

Technology Production: Jamie Kostecki, Paola Ríos Schaaf

Design: Robin Herr, Michelle Ingari, Jhoany Jiménez, Nick Ventullo

Production: Oscar Díez, Jennifer López, Lina Lozano, Fabian Montoya, Andrés Vanegas

Student Text ISBN: 978-1-61857-895-2

Instructor's Annotated Edition ISBN: 978-1-61857-898-3

Library of Congress Control Number: 2013950421

8 9 TC 19

Printed in Canada.

Introduction

Welcome to **¡ADELANTE!, Second Edition**. This three-volume introductory Spanish program is designed to provide you with an active and rewarding learning experience. You have an exciting journey through the Spanish language and the Spanish-speaking world ahead of you.

NEW to the Second Edition

- A dynamic new **Fotonovela**, filmed in the Yucatan Peninsula and Mexico City, that presents language and culture in an engaging context
- Enhanced Supersite—a simplified, user-friendly interface that highlights current assignments and makes all resources easy to find
- iPad®-friendly* access—get Supersite on the go!
- Online chat activities for synchronous communication and oral practice—2 per lesson
- New **A primera vista** questions that use previously learned vocabulary and grammar to ask about lesson opener photos
- 3 new **Lectura** readings, plus Supersite audio-sync technology for all **Lectura** readings
- Expanded **Adelante** skill-building section, with new **Escritura**, **Escuchar**, **En pantalla**, and **Flash cultura** pages for each lesson
- New audio for activities on **Escuchar** pages
- New **En pantalla** TV clips and short films showcasing Spanish from diverse locations in the Spanish-speaking world
- In-text integration of the enormously successful **Flash cultura**
- An expanded Testing Program with new tests, plus vocabulary and grammar quizzes

Plus, the original hallmark features of ¡ADELANTE!

- Easy-to-carry, spiral-bound worktext with perforated pages and folders
- Inclusion of Workbook, Video Manual, and Lab Manual pages at the end of each worktext lesson
- Review lessons at the beginning of **¡ADELANTE! DOS** and **¡ADELANTE! TRES**
- Additional Vocabulary and Notes pages at the end of each lesson
- Tabs and color coding for ease of navigation
- Clear and concise grammar and vocabulary sections
- Two compelling cultural videos: **Flash cultura** and **Panorama cultural**

*Students must use a computer for audio recording and select presentations and tools that require Flash or Shockwave.

table of contents

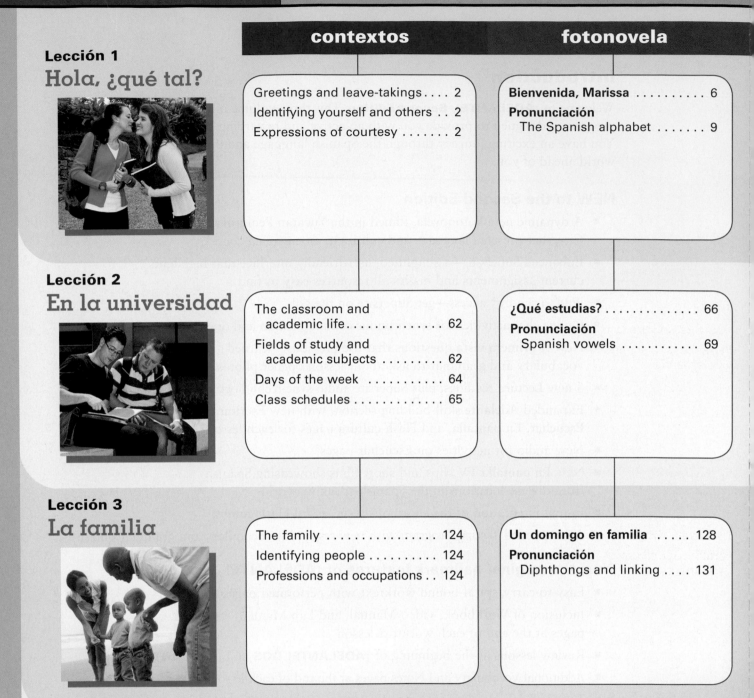

cultura	estructura	adelante

	contextos	**fotonovela**

Lección 4
Los pasatiempos

Lección 5
Las vacaciones

Lección 6
¡De compras!

Ancillaries

cultura	estructura	adelante

Consulta

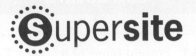
Super**site**

Each section of your worktext comes with activities on the **¡ADELANTE!** Supersite, many of which are auto-graded for immediate feedback. Plus, the Supersite is iPad®-friendly*, so it can be accessed on the go! Visit **vhlcentral.com** to explore this wealth of exciting resources.

CONTEXTOS
- Vocabulary tutorials
- Image-based vocabulary activity with audio
- Audio activities
- Worktext activities
- Additional activities for extra practice
- Chat activities for conversational skill-building and oral practice

FOTONOVELA
- Streaming video of **Fotonovela**, with instructor-managed options for subtitles and transcripts in Spanish and English
- Worktext activities
- Additional activities for extra practice
- Audio files for **Pronunciación**
- Record-compare practice

CULTURA
- Reading available online
- Keywords and support for **Conexión Internet**
- Worktext activities
- Additional activities for extra practice
- Additional reading

ESTRUCTURA
- Animated grammar tutorials
- Grammar presentations available online
- Worktext activities
- Additional activities for extra practice
- Chat activities for conversational skill-building and oral practice
- Diagnostics in **Recapitulación** section

ADELANTE
- Audio-synced reading in **Lectura**
- Additional reading
- Writing activity in **Escritura** with composition engine
- Audio files for listening activity in **Escuchar**
- Worktext activities and additional activities for extra practice
- Streaming **En pantalla** TV clips or short films, with instructor-managed options for subtitles and transcripts in Spanish and English
- Streaming video of **Flash cultura** series, with instructor-managed options for subtitles and transcripts in Spanish and English

VOCABULARIO
- Vocabulary list with audio
- Flashcards with audio

PANORAMA
- Interactive map
- Worktext activities
- Additional activities for extra practice
- Streaming video of **Panorama cultural** series, with instructor-managed options for subtitles and transcripts in Spanish and English

Plus! Also found on the Supersite:

- All worktext and lab audio MP3 files
- Communication center for instructor notifications and feedback
- Live Chat tool for video chat, audio chat, and instant messaging without leaving your browser
- A single gradebook for all Supersite activities
- WebSAM online Workbook/Video Manual and Lab Manual

*Students must use a computer for audio recording and select presentations and tools that require Flash or Shockwave.

Icons and *Recursos* boxes

Icons

Familiarize yourself with these icons that appear throughout **¡ADELANTE!, Second Edition**.

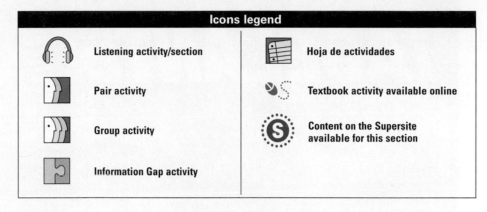

Icons legend	
Listening activity/section	Hoja de actividades
Pair activity	Textbook activity available online
Group activity	Content on the Supersite available for this section
Information Gap activity	

- Additional practice on the Supersite, not included in the worktext, is indicated with this icon:

  Practice more at **vhlcentral.com**.

Recursos

Recursos boxes let you know exactly what print and technology ancillaries you can use to reinforce and expand on every section of the lessons in your worktext. They even include page numbers when applicable.

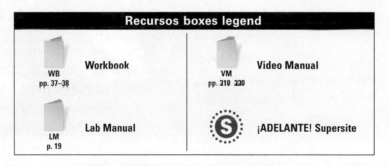

Recursos boxes legend	
WB pp. 37–38 — Workbook	VM pp. 210 330 — Video Manual
LM p. 19 — Lab Manual	¡ADELANTE! Supersite

Student Ancillaries

- **Workbook/Video Manual/Lab Manual**
  All of these materials are available right inside your worktext, at the end of each lesson.
- **Lab Audio Program**
  The audio files to accompany the Lab Manual are available on the Supersite.
- **Worktext Audio Program MP3s**
  The Worktext Audio Program MP3s, available on the Supersite, are the audio recordings for the listening-based activities and recordings of the active vocabulary in each lesson of the **¡ADELANTE!** program.
- **WebSAM**
  The WebSAM delivers the Workbook, Video Manual, and Lab Manual online.

Worktext Format
delivers materials in a convenient, user-friendly package.

Spiral binding A unique binding allows easier handling of materials in class, at home, or wherever you may be.

Perforation Perforated pages allow you to easily hand in assignments or travel with just what you need.

Folders and notes For your convenience, folders and note papers are included.

Tab navigation Clearly marked tabs ensure that you always know exactly where you are in the worktext.

Built-in ancillaries The Workbook, Video Manual, and Lab Manual activities are included after each worktext lesson, eliminating the need to carry these components to and from class.